KAKADU
REFLECTIONS

KAKADU
REFLECTIONS

BRUCE PREWER

with photography by
IAN MORRIS

LEFT: *Kakadu escarpment near East Alligator River*

Lutheran Publishing House

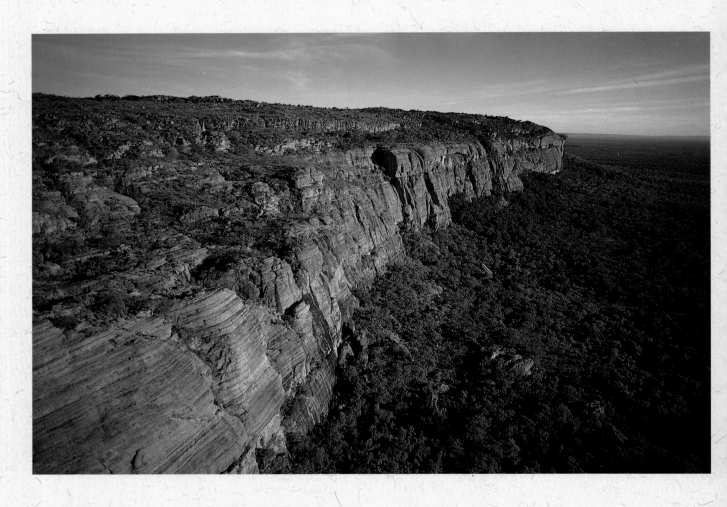

First printing August 1988
Second printing November 1988
Third printing July 1989

National Library of Australia Cataloguing-in-Publication data

Prewer, Bruce D. (Bruce David), 1931-
 Kakadu reflections.

 ISBN 0 85910 467 2.

 1. Christian poetry, Australian. 2. Kakadu National Park (N.T.) — Poetry.
 I. Morris, Ian, 1951- II. Title.

A821'.3

Printed by Griffin Press, Adelaide.

Published by Lutheran Publishing House,
205 Halifax Street, Adelaide, South Australia. LPH 89-758

INTRODUCTION

By an act of grace — a rare thing in this greedy world — Kakadu is there for us all to enjoy, thanks to the Aboriginal owners. Having first fought to establish their rights as owners, with typical generosity they leased the area back to the National Parks and Wildlife Service in November 1978 so that we could all come and appreciate their home country.

The Park is about 220 kilometres east of Darwin, and consists of 19,000 square kilometres of tidal flats, floodplain, lowlands, and plateau country. Features that stand out are rivers, billabongs, and waterfalls (in the wet season), and especially the rugged, sandstone uplands of the Arnhem Land escarpment. Kakadu has many faces, many moods, and is home to a multitude of life-forms.

To the casual eye, much of the Park appears to be uninteresting bushland and savannah grassland, with gum trees and occasional stands of palms. What seems to make it even more uninteresting for some folk is that during the dry season many areas are deliberately burned, leaving them charred and smoking, with kites circling overhead looking for prey. But to the trained eye, all is not as it seems. The unspectacular bushland is home to a complex plant and animal kingdom which merges with and relates to the sedgland, the paper bark forests, the mangroves, monsoon forests, and the woodlands of the plateau. All are parts of one tapestry. Even the burning-off follows an ancient Aboriginal rotational system which does not destroy life, but stimulates and protects it.

LEFT: *Lightning Dreaming (Namarrkurn)*
UPPER RIGHT: *Indjuwanydjuwa painting*
LOWER RIGHT: *White-breasted Sea Eagle*

Kakadu is a rare survivor. It is one part of the 'top end' of Australia which as yet has not suffered irreparable damage from European settlement. Plant and animal life are generally intact. Those who visit this National Park are seeing a part of Australia almost as it has been for thousands of years — and that is precious! It imparts a sense of timelessness which is absent in our cities and in much of our devegetated countryside.

Wildlife is prolific in Kakadu. Tourists get excited by large flocks of magpie geese, whistling ducks, or pygmy geese. They stand amazed at trees so covered with cockatoos or parrots that they seem like trees in full blossom. The elegant stork, the jabiru, catches the attention as it wades in shallow waters gathering food. But what is noticed is only a small part of the population of 275 bird species which frequent this region.

Reptiles also come into the abundant category. There are 75 species, of which the usual visitor sees but a few. It is the crocodiles which provide most interest. Freshwater streams and billabongs are the habitat of the small Johnston crocodiles, shy and elusive.

However, it is the big saltwater crocs that most people come to see. They are tender parents, formidable hunters, and possess a speed and agility which is amazing in such bulky creatures. Although their habitat is usually the saltwater areas, they are also found in some streams and billabongs elsewhere, even as far as Jim Jim Falls. The wisest way to get a close look at these leviathans in the wild is in the company of guided tours for this purpose. The Rangers rightly warn that, because the crocodiles have not been hunted for many years, they are losing the fear of human

beings. Visitors are well advised to take no risks by staying clear of them.

Although crocodiles and birds are the most easily seen in Kakadu's wildlife, there are 50 species of mammal, 25 of frogs, and 55 of fish — to say nothing of the many colourful and spectacular insects which fly, crawl, and swim during various seasons. In fact, it is the prodigal dimension to the variety and abundance of life in Kakadu which leaves one quite overwhelmed.

Wildlife Service have provided walking tracks and information about art styles and mythology. Beside the fascination of the changing art styles, there are surprises. At Ubirr one can see the painting of a Tasmanian Tiger, or of European visitors who came into the region in the last century — complete with rifles in their hands, and pipes in their mouths! Experts say that the art styles found in the area span a period of about 20,000 years — something one cannot find anywhere else in the world. Such art sites are a national treasure. They link us with the long, long story of humanity. Australians are, indeed, an ancient and spiritual people.

Over 250 of the descendants of those ancient artists still live within the boundaries of the Park. Most are out of sight, glad to see others enjoying their country, but reluctant to be on the tourist agenda themselves! Some have become well-trained and much-valued Rangers, keen to help visitors explore, understand, and appreciate the place which they love and treasure like a mother.

The most stunning land-form is the great, 500-kilometre-long Arnhem Land escarpment, with its buttresses, pillars, cliffs, and outliers (the remains of the plateau which centuries of erosion have left standing out on the lowlands). The weather has sculptured much of the sandstone into intriguing shapes. To be in the stone country near dawn or dusk, when the rock is radiant with colour, is among the special experiences which Kakadu can offer.

For many residents and visitors, the most notable and profound aspect of Kakadu is the Aboriginal heritage, including over 6,000 rock art sites. Kakadu is a people place. Archeologists who have examined some of the old camp-sites claim that the human story goes back at least 23,000 years, perhaps even 50,000. To be able to visit and stand within an ancient camp-site, such as the Anbangbang Shelter, can be an exciting and awesome experience.

Two of the best-known, and most-accessible, rock art sites are at Ubirr in the north, and at Nourlangie in the south, where the Parks and

Of course, a visitor can see only a little, and understand even less. For fuller familiarity one would need to stay there often, to experience the changing moods and seasons. The thunder and lightning displays of November are a vivid contrast to the clear days of June. The dry, dusty lowlands and dried-up wetlands of August-September are almost another world compared with the torrential rain and waterways of December-March. Only those who actually reside at Kakadu can really begin to understand its many treasures. That is not possible for most of us —nor is it desirable for the Park!

Kakadu is not for everyone. Some tourists come and go, wondering what all the excitement is about. Bored to tears, they can hardly wait to get back to the bustle of Sydney, New York, or Tokyo. That is not surprising, for Kakadu is a place with a special, subtle quality which is hard to define. Some call it a spiritual quality. It is there for those who approach it gently, respectfully, and with time to absorb its mystique.

Whatever glimmers of appreciation I have for Kakadu National Park are largely due to Ian Morris, a Park Officer whose photography is featured in this volume. Ian has a profound affection and respect for the land and its people. He also has a deep and abiding love for the Creator. One can sense these qualities in the pages of this volume.

Together we present *Kakadu Reflections* with gratitude to the One who has provided places like Kakadu.

Easter 1988

Bruce Prewer,
Pilgrim Church, Adelaide

HOW MUCH MORE

If my eye is excited
by teeming life
in due season,
   how much more
    by the abundant Life
    of all seasons.

If my ear delights
in the song
of a butcher bird
at dawn,
   how much more
    in the love-song
    of the Spirit.

If the handiwork
is awesomely beautiful
beyond words,
   how much more
    the beauty
    of the Hands.

UPPER LEFT: *Sorghum seed-head*
LOWER LEFT: *Lotus at Cannon Hill Billabong*
RIGHT: *Grey-backed Butcher Bird singing at dawn*

SUNRISE IN STONE COUNTRY

Sandstone outliers
lift their rugged turrets
through the enchanting dawn
like castles of another kingdom.

The dependable old sun
pushes his way up
over the great escarpment
and touches peaks with red gold.

Bats take shelter in caves,
agile wallabies seek rest
on the rocky slopes,
termites begin relentless labour.

It's time for the singing of the birds:
the bar-shouldered dove,
the call of the honeyeater,
the strident joy of the kookaburra.

Now the light reaches the lowlands,
the distant swamps and billabongs,
glazing across bird-lined waters
and suffusing lush grasses and reeds.

This one small parcel of creation
is awake with the glory of a new day —
awake to serve the Wisdom that made it
and the Love that sustains it!

LEFT: *Blue-winged Kookaburra*
RIGHT: *Kakadu Dawn from Jabiru Dreaming (Djagarna)*

THE DOVE

Dove in the stone country
calling at daybreak.
Sign of the Mystery,
Spirit of love.

Dove among mangroves,
enjoying the morning.
Sign of belonging,
Spirit of love.

Dove over waters,
descending like light.
Sign of the Holy One,
Spirit of love.

LOVE-LIGHT

God, the most holy,
God, the most beautiful,
said:
Let there be light.
And it was so.

Star-light glistening
    on smooth rock pools.
Moon-light caressing
    lilies in billabongs.
Green-light filtering
    to forest floors.
White-light viewed
    from the mouth of a cave.
Fierce-light bouncing
    off rockcliffs at noon.
Multi-light flashing
    on a swooping rainbow bird.
Dusk-light gentling
    over wide floodplains.
Dawn-light cresting
    over many-tiered stone country.

Love-light embracing
    all things,
    all people,
from you, most glorious God!
Aflame is the world
    with your glory!
Alight are your people
    with holy joy!

UPPER LEFT: *Bar-shouldered Doves*
LOWER LEFT: *Djuwarr Billabong, Deaf Adder Gorge*
UPPER RIGHT: *Kakadu wetlands in flood, South Alligator River*
LOWER RIGHT: *Light through leaves*

UPPER: *Glossy Ibis, Yellow Waters*
LOWER: *South Alligator floodplain (Gumunkuwuy)*

NEAR EDEN?

A small cloud of pigmy geese take wing,
wheeling over the wetlands,
green-sheening in the afternoon sun.

Watching us, yet not alarmed,
bulky magpie geese, legs red-knobbly,
stand massed in the shallows.

A light wind dusts the water's face
and ruffles the heads of tall grasses
which stretch to where paper barks stand tall.

Now a tribe of Burdekin ducks,
brown backs sloping, glistening,
twist necks, warily watching.

Glossy ibis pretend we are not here
as they stalk around the margins
with sickle-beaks ready for prey.

Their neighbours, more distant, the egrets,
outstretch elegant white necks
and stand like Michelangelo marble.

A gross of whistling ducks catch panic,
rise like a swarm of offended bees
and flurry away to the east.

Some tall jabiru, reserved and remote,
keep stalking up and down a mudbank
out in the swamp near a mangrove.

All the while, lotus birds
in pairs mime messiah convincingly
across weed and lily leaves.

My senses are in a tumult of joy
at the liberality of it all!
Am I somewhere near Eden?

O Wonderful is your name, loving Creator!
Blessed are the works of your hands!

FIRST THINGS FIRST

Asleep in the folds of night,
long have I joyfully dreamed
the wonder of flight.

Yet next day I am found
plodding, and sometimes crawling,
across the lowly ground.

Lord, take not away
the glory of that dream
as I begin each day.

But tell me surely
that walking truly
across uneven soil
without despairing
is faith's
first goal.

KNOWING

The jabiru knows her world
    and is nourished in abundance.
The turtle and swallow read seasons.
    And the brolga knows when to rejoice.

But do we yet read the times
    and know the possibilities in change?
Do we discern the winds
    and love the mystery of light?

Come, day of fulfilment —
    when knowledge is inward written,
and from the greatest to the least
    all shall know their inheritance!

(Inspired by Jeremiah 8:7 & 31:34)

UPPER LEFT: *White-breasted Sea Eagle*
FAR LEFT: *Pied Stilt, Bamboo Creek*
NEARER LEFT: *Magpie Geese on Angurrapal Billabong*
UPPER RIGHT: *Female Jabiru, Yellow Waters*
LOWER RIGHT: *Short-necked Turtle*
OVERLEAF: *Malangangerr*

SEEING GOD

God is on the waters,
   God is in the land,
God is on the mountain,
   God is in your hand.

God is in the forest,
   God is on the plain,
God is in the desert,
   God is in your brain.

God is in the sunlight,
   God is in the air,
God is on a falcon's wing,
   God is in your prayer.

God is in our laughter,
   God is in sad loss.
God is in forgiveness,
   God is on the Cross.

LEFT: *Gulungul Creek, Mt Brockman*
UPPER RIGHT: *Deaf Adder Gorge from Djuwarr*
LOWER RIGHT: *Jim Jim Falls*

LOVE'S ENERGY

Your energy, O Lord, is infinite,
    your authority everlasting.
You divide many rivers,
    you thunder in the waterfall,
you surge in the flood,
    and even tame the crocodile.

Yet you have many enemies —
    numerous in our land —
fools who mock your existence,
    or mix your name with obscenities.

Save us, O Lord, from their power,
    deliver us from their wounding.
We are in their midst like peaceful doves
    surrounded by fierce hawks.

O Lord, rescue all who are endangered;
    remember the homeless poor.
You alone are True God,
    Love from the very beginning,
Friend of living creatures,
    Saviour of all people!

UPPER LEFT: *Escarpment pool*
LOWER LEFT: *Saltwater Crocodile, East Alligator River*
RIGHT: *Twin Falls*

(Inspired by Psalm 74:12–20)

WATER LILY

The good Lord said
to his most skilful
angel:

Take a billabong,
grow some slender paper barks
on one side,
and place
a red-rock face
on the other.
Then add tall reeds
where fowl may nest.

Now within the water
fashion a special plant
with long limbs,
and leaves
wider than hands,
on which birds may walk.

Then carefully
raise from the roots
of this plant
a long, firm stem
on which to set
a matchless flower
in due season.

Let the sun
at dawn or dusk
outline the flower's
pure shape,
and tint it with colour
from the lips
of cherubim.

LEFT: *Buywek Goluy Billabong*
UPPER RIGHT: *Water Lily* (Nymphaea violacea)
LOWER RIGHT: *Young Lotus Bird, Yellow Waters*

For eyes not yet created
shall one day come,
discover,
and marvel
at this fair
but faint reflection
of amazing grace.

MORNING

Whatever the Lord does,
he does well
through mountain and valley
on floodplain and billabong.

He makes the morning mist
rise around sandstone outliers.
He sends the wallaby to rest,
and wakes the dove and kingfisher.
He tints the peaks with crimson,
and calls the world to worship.

Let all who have eyes to see,
let all who have ears to hear,
greet the Lord
who does all things well!

UPPER LEFT: *Forest Kingfisher*
LOWER LEFT: *View from Jabiru Dreaming (Djagarna)*
UPPER RIGHT: *'From plateau to plain' (Djuwarr)*
LOWER RIGHT: *Great Egret*

PRAYER OF THE DUST

Come, dayspring from on high,
come to your own
and fashion a generation
of seers.

Spread the dawn
over grey horizons,
and prepare eyes
for the first light.

Come as you came
on a cloud of yesterdays,
and touch the dust
with a radiant image.

SIMPLE HAPPINESS

Is not this happiness:
To rise in the company
    of a good friend;
to eat a simple breakfast
    with gratitude;
to say one's prayers
    outdoors in the sun
    with a rowdy choir
    of red-collared lorikeets;
to pick up a book without haste
    and savour rich meditations
    from wise ones
    who lived long ago;
to remember loved ones
    far away or near;
to know it is the very truth
    when the Nazarene says:
    'Be of good cheer'.

UPPER: *Red-collared Lorikeets*
LOWER: *Eucalyptus ptychocarpa (Malangangerr)*

MONSOON

Sound in our ears
   like a mighty rushing wind;
Light in our eyes
   like tongues of lightning;
New breath in our lungs
   like the gift of a Risen One;

Then weariness is washed away
and everything sings with joy
at the renewing of life.

LOWER: *Kapok Tree at Umuwal, East Alligator River*
OVERLEAF: *Magpie Geese, Yellow Waters*

MUDDY FEET

When events
flow sluggishly,
forcing me
to spend time
in muddy places,

Lord,
give me the grace
to make use
of mud
as successfully
as does
the mangrove.

LEFT: *Dead Mangrove Forest*
RIGHT: *Mangrove Tree, East Alligator Mouth*

NONE SO BLIND?

O eye of Australian,
beguiled by the movements
on the stock exchange,
can't you see
the 'many-splendoured thing'?

O eye of Australian,
lured with the fiction
and fashion of self-fulfilment,
can't you see
the surge of the Spirit?

O eye of Australian,
programmed for lust
and lost in its wasteland,
can't you see
the light of Life?

LEFT: *Oenpelli Primary School children at Cannon Hill Billabong*
UPPER RIGHT: *Monsoon Forest Spiny Spider*
LOWER RIGHT: *Children playing in the Arafura Sea*

THE WORD

This whole world
is a remarkable word
spoken by a Lover
into the darkness.

Within that word
many small words:
some passive
like stones,
some beautiful
like orchids,
some surprising
like python patterns,
some perplexing
like hunted perchlets.

Mightier, and loveliest,
one incomparable Word
was enfleshed
among us;
a word far greater
than the world
of which it is a part,
yet leaving nothing —
not one fragment —
untouched
by its glory.

UPPER LEFT: *Fungus growing out of mossy tree trunk, monsoon forest*
LOWER LEFT: *The Rare Red-eye Butterfly, Arnhem Land*
UPPER RIGHT: *Nawaran, the Oenpelli Python*
LOWER RIGHT: *Cannon Hill view*

UPPER LEFT: *Open woodland fire (Mambirri)*
LOWER LEFT: *Freshwater Mangrove flowers*
UPPER RIGHT: *View from Bluetongue Dreaming*
LOWER RIGHT: *Sandstone Melaleuca flower*

THE TIME OF FIRES

Lord, my stiff mind
finds it hard to accept
that fire is your servant.

Our black folk say
it is the necessary agent
for life, old and new.

But for white folk,
zealous in dodging discomfort,
fire seems offensive.

Yet my own eyes witness
to the vigorous greening
that follows the flames.

That flames can be
an expression of love,
Lord, help me to believe.

NEARNESS

Near is the Mind
which frames all,
  limitless
    for ever the same
    for ever changing.

Near is the Power
which leavens all,
  limitless
    for ever covenanting
    for ever free.

Near is the Love
which embraces all,
  limitless
    for ever perfect suffering
    for ever perfect joy.

Near is the Nearness
which is our dreaming,
  limitless
    for ever our quest
    for ever our rest.

LORD OF THE STORM

At tranquil dawn
I dare not profess you,
unless within the storm
I also confess you.

In friend
I cannot claim you,
unless in enemy
I also name you.

Healthy, I dare not
say I know you,
unless diseased
I still adore you.

Nowhere shall I
truly greet you,
unless upon the Cross
I meet you.

UPPER LEFT: *Cannon Hill Billabong*
LOWER LEFT: *Agile Wallaby (Gonobolo) and young at foot, open woodland*
RIGHT: *Storm north of Cannon Hill*
OVERLEAF: *Saltwater Crocodile, Yellow Waters*

CREATURES OF LIGHT

And the Word was:
'Let there be light —
the sun to rule by day,
the moon and stars by night.'

God made things to enjoy it:
butterflies, buffaloes, and bees,
eagles riding on the wind,
and turtles in the seas.

Then God took some clay,
and said: 'Now, this is fun!'
He gave it the kiss of life
and placed it in the sun.

Up into life it leapt —
child, woman, man.
God said: 'Now, this is good,
the best since things began.'

'Now, this is good
by day or night,
now, this is good,
creatures of light!'

UPPER LEFT: *Yellow Lilies, Magela Creek*
LOWER LEFT: *Bull, Asian Water Buffalo*
RIGHT: *Kevin Buliwana, Deaf Adder Gorge*

EMMAUS

If this collection
of shapes and colours
were life's only light,
sole ground of faith,
   how wretched
    we would be.

If we must deduce
from this alone
the first cause
and the final goal,
   how confused
    we would be.

If you, Lord,
had not met us
on the way
and opened the Scriptures,
   how lost
    we would be.

LEFT: *Gulungul Creek forest*
UPPER RIGHT: *Gould's Goanna*
LOWER RIGHT: *Aldjurr, the Leichhardt's
Grasshopper*

THANKS FOR THE COMICAL

For all things bright and beautiful,
we thank you, loving Creator,
but also for the surprise and delight
of creatures odd and comical:

Embarrassed-looking goanna
tree-wrapped above the floods.

Cumbersome crocodile diving
without splash or ripple.

Willy wagtail in angry display
ejecting a trespassing kite.

Curled-up death adder
imitating a crocheted scarf.

Great bower-bird rushing around
like a bossy school prefect.

Spiny anteater sunbaking
on its back and snoring.

Lotus birds on the waters
busily playing messiah.

White spoonbills earnestly shovelling
like labourers on a muddy building site.

Bulky buffalo bull threatening
but making a noise like a piglet.

Thank you, Lord, for giving us
eyes to see them,
lips to tell,
and the capacity to laugh!

UPPER LEFT: *Lotus Bird*
LOWER LEFT: *Crocodile*
RIGHT: *Goanna stranded in flood*

THE RAINS

Freely our praise comes to you, O God,
    worshipping in response to your faithfulness.

You visit the earth and water it,
    you come among us with refreshment.
You soften the hills with rains,
    and quench their thirst with storms.
The rivers of God are overflowing,
    the soil is prepared for new growth.
Creeks and swamps are renewed,
    waterfalls thunder with joy!

You crown the year with gladness,
    all your footsteps drip with new life —
life for wilderness places,
    till the mountain slopes are green,
flocks gather on the plains,
    and flowers carpet the bushland.

UPPER LEFT: *Dew on Flagallaria*
LOWER LEFT: *Djabiluku area, Magela Creek*
UPPER RIGHT: *Twin Falls*
LOWER RIGHT: *Buywek Goluy Billabong*

There is an ear that hears our prayers,
  a love to whom all can turn.
You give us joy at the break of day,
  and fill the evenings with happiness.
Everything declares its exaltation!
Everything is a song of highest praise!

(Echoing Psalm 65)

ROOTS

Your people, Lord,
and my people:
from the same dust
of Australian soil
you have fashioned us
to be one family.

Your people, Lord,
and my true people:
in their insights
and long, long story
in this timeless land
are found my true roots.

Their ancestors,
enjoying rock and creek,
reptile and bird,
sunrise and sunset,
ages before we came,
are my story.

My every rejection
or denigration
even to the least of these,
any paternalistic phrase,
severs me, maimed,
from deep-down springs.

Lord, have mercy.
Save your new Australians
from myopic madness.
Give us the humility
to allow them
to teach us many things.

LEFT: *Bombax trees on South Alligator River*
UPPER RIGHT: *Nipper Gabirriki at Djuwarr Gallery*
LOWER RIGHT: *Magela catchment*
OVERLEAF: *Upper East Alligator River*

TRIBAL SITE

This is a joyful
and wonder-full thing:
to stand hushed
where a great people
lived continuously
from ancient days.

To be a brief part
of a noble stream,
generations onflowing
of precious
communal life
in this place.

How many
campfire meals?
How many happy tales
of a day's hunt?
Or the mighty deeds
of ancestors?

What wounds
of body or spirit
have been tended here?
What loving looks
silently exchanged,
or babies suckled?

Now we come, unworthy,
yet inheritors,
if we are willing
to humbly approach
and deeply respect
this stone cathedral.

Surely the Lord
is in this place,
yet we, in blindness,
knew it not. Now
how great the awe!
Lord, how great the awe!

LEFT: *Djuwarr, Deaf Adder Valley*
UPPER RIGHT: *Speared Kangaroo, Manngolin Gallery*
LOWER RIGHT: *Banama Gallery (Djirringbal)*

JESUS WEPT

I found him sobbing,
   Jesus, the one called Christ,
sitting on a stone ledge
in the large empty space
under a sloping overhang
   at Burrungguy.

He did not heed me,
   Jesus, the one called Christ,
but kept staring at walls,
fingering grinding holes,
brooding over the vacancy
   at Burrungguy.

He knew as a brother,
   Jesus, the one called Christ,
the inner meaning of this place
where once camp-fires glowed
for thousands of years
   at Burrungguy.

Never again, he knew,
   Jesus, the one called Christ,
never again the fires and soft chatter,
food, love, and laughter,
nor the songs of Namarrkurn
   at Burrungguy.

I left him weeping,
   Jesus, the one called Christ;
unable to watch with him
beyond a while in such grief —
or with such fierce love —
   at Burrungguy.

LEFT: *Malangangerr*
RIGHT: *Joseph Giradbul, Inyalak Gallery*

FOR EVERYTHING A PLACE

In the sandstone country
I hear the song
of the white-lined honeyeater,
   and know
    it belongs.

At the river's edge
I see the crocodile
basking in sunshine,
   and know
    it belongs.

Across the lowlands
I see a flock of pelicans
in thick formation,
   and know
    they belong.

Watching from the peak
of an ancient rock
we wait for Sunday's dawn,
   and know
    we belong.

UPPER LEFT: *Crocodile*
LOWER LEFT: *East Alligator Valley area*
RIGHT: *White-throated Honeyeaters*

FOR THE MEEK

Wonderful is our humble Lord,
  friend of all the earth.
The whole world is his own,
  filled with unquenchable light.
He upholds the poor of the land,
and saves the children of the needy.

He comes like living water,
  like rains renewing the dusty earth.
Goodness fills his days,
  peace flows by without limit.
Low places provide fruit in plenty,
  even rocky places grow sweet fruits.

Then shall the lonely outback
  gladly bow before him.
Leaders not yet born
  shall freely serve him.
Precious shall his blood be
  in the hearts of all his people.

Longer than the sun shall rule
  across land and sea by day,
longer than the moon shall shine
  across the bushland by night,
the meek shall sing his name,
  and trust his utter love.

LEFT: Cindi Cooper, Wildman River
UPPER RIGHT: Rock Possum, Little Nawulandja Rock
LOWER RIGHT: Djarrdjarr Billabong, Magela Creek

THE BLUES

Lord, I have bad days
   when I pray without hearing,
and nights of grave disquiet
   when my hand reaches into darkness.
I try to meditate,
   but it makes things worse.
I complain and protest
   without relieving my discontent.

On such overcast days I wonder:
   Has God withdrawn his love?
I say to myself:
   Was my faith ever real?
Were the sacred promises an illusion?
   Is the Spirit a fiction?

Then, Lord, you bring me to my senses:
   I refuse to bow to my feelings.
I say: The Lord is God
   whether I feel him or not;
I am surely baptized,
   no matter what oppresses me.
I am God's child,
   and Christ has died to prove it!

(Inspired by Psalm 77:1–12)

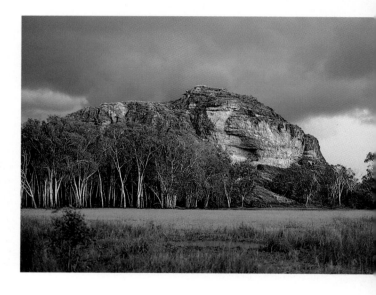

UPPER LEFT: *East Alligator Floodplain* (Nardab)
LOWER LEFT: *Jabiru Dreaming* (Djagarna)
RIGHT: *Riflefish Dreaming* (Nyarlgan)

GLORY

Glory be to you, Lord,
for you have given us creation
with its colours and shapes,
sounds and tastes.

Glory be to you, Lord,
for you have given the human family
with its many tongues and cultures.

Glory be to you, Lord,
for you have given us Christ Jesus,
brother of each, and redeemer of all.

Therefore, with all loving people,
near or far off,
remembered or forgotten,
we join to praise you:

Holy, holy, holy Lord of joy,
the earth and the heavens are full
of the radiance of your glory.
Glory be to you,
friend most lovable,
Lord most wonderful!

THE PRESENCE

Lord,
sometimes the air
seems charged
with your Presence,
saturated,
pulsing,
like a music
composed of
pure love.

Then it is
that the panting soul
is wondrously quietened,
for our dearest self
can breathe well
on even a little
of this atmosphere.

LEFT: *Lilies, post-wet season, Buywek Goluy Billabong*
UPPER RIGHT: *Magela Creek Lily*
LOWER RIGHT: *Grevillea pteridifolia*
OVERLEAF: *Main escarpment (Namarrkurn)*

IF YOU HAVE BREATH

Let everyone praise the Lord of life.
Let all things praise the Lord of love.

Give praise in your churches,
sound your praise in open places:
    with the grace of the great egret,
    with the ease of the eagle,
    with the tenacity of the turtle,
    with the courage of the crocodile.

Sound your happiness, bugling brolga.
Give praise, chirping crimson finch.
Come all who have ears to hear.
Come all who have songs to sing:
Let everything that draws breath,
praise our most wonderful God!

(Inspired by Psalm 146)

LEFT: *Great Egret, Wetlands*
UPPER RIGHT: *White-breasted Sea Eagle*
LOWER RIGHT: *Snake-necked Turtle*

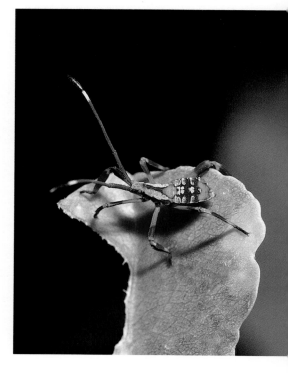

UPPER LEFT: *Assassin Bug*
LOWER LEFT: *Sandstone-dwelling tree frog*
UPPER RIGHT: *Morning Glory* (Ipomoea abrupta)
LOWER RIGHT: *Monsoon Forest Fly*

FROM BUSYNESS

Lord, save me
from the busyness
that fails to see

your beauty
in every bush and tree,

your power
in every plant and flower,

your love
in all the things
that live and move,
including me.

THE UNSPEAKABLE

There is a Truth
about which I cannot speak
without mistelling it.
Its treasure I cannot share
without shortselling it.

Its secret
seems less than a mustard seed,
yet shakes the mountains.
Its light
seems less than a moonbeam,
yet fills the world.

This Truth
cannot be grasped
by the greedy and proud.
The humble who live it
will truly know it.

LEFT: *Water Lily* (Nymphaea violacea)
UPPER RIGHT: *Sunset over Magela Creek*
LOWER RIGHT: *View from Nawurrkpil*

WHERE WERE YOU?

Where were you, mere human,
    when living creatures were formed?
What did you amount to
    when bird and beast took shape?
Did you play with the first native cat
    or feed the shy sugar glider?
Where were you when the python arrived,
    or when the butcher bird first sang?

You had no part in constructing the crocodile,
    you were not needed to draw the plans.
Watch it there on the reedy mudbank,
    see it basking in the sun.
What massive strength is in its body,
    what power is in its great muscles!
The tail is as sturdy as a gum tree,
    it fells animals like lightning.
Its bones are like steel pipes,
    its legs are as pile-drivers.
On its back there is a row of shields,
    an armour hard to pierce.
The jaws are lined with daggers;
    they close like an iron vice.
Its nostrils blow forth steam,
    its eyes gleam like the dawn.

Where were you, mere human,
    when living creatures were formed?
You had no thought in their designing,
    you had no hand in their nurturing.
Be humbled, and consider the Purpose that planned,
    the Power that devised and sustains.
O worship the Lord in the midst of creation!
    Serve him as you treasure his handiwork!

(Echoing Job 38 – 40)

UPPER LEFT: *Little Northern Quoll*
LOWER LEFT: *Saltwater Crocodile*
RIGHT: *Northern Sugar Glider*

SIMPLE PSALM

The sun shines freely on all things,
   the craft of God is displayed.

How complete are all creatures,
   how delightful to the seeing eye.
They go their way each morning,
   each fulfilling a simple destiny.
They move in pairs or flocks,
   each complementing the other.

Who can grow bored with such a world,
   who can tire of its many patterns?
Who can grow weary of discerning
   the fingerprints of a greater Glory?

UPPER LEFT: *Rainbow Bee-eater*
LOWER LEFT: *Robber Fly*
RIGHT: *Whistling Ducks, Yellow Waters*

EPHPHATHA

I begged a word.
But the whistling kite
and the cuckoo shrike
were all I heard.

I craved a sign.
But a swamp hen's nest
and a spoonbill's crest
were only mine.

I asked God why?
In the silence that came
he whispered my name
as the wind went by.

I knew it then:
In eyes that are clear,
in ears that hear,
he is present again.

LEFT: *Braminy Kite*
UPPER RIGHT: *Habernaria Orchid*
LOWER RIGHT: *Red-collared Lorikeet*
OVERLEAF: *Mt Brockman (Djidbidjidbi)*

THIS TEMPLE

How lovely is your living place,
   Joy of all creation!
My body and mind praise you,
   all that I am delights in you!

Like the woodswallow I have a home,
   a nest in dependable rock:
among these open chapels,
   these altars under the sun
shaped by your loving hands,
   my friend and my God.

Happy are those who recognize this temple;
   joyful shall be their worship.
Happy are those who know your strength;
   they shall love your ways.

Even in a valley of tears
   they shall find hope.
Threatening storms
   will bring new life.
Your friends grow in strength,
   securely grounded in you.

God of the universe, you hear each prayer,
   God of my forebears, you turn your ear.
One day walking with you
   is better than a thousand alone.

I would rather be your poorest child
   than a rebel living in luxury.
Your love shines brighter than sunlight,
   transfiguring all things.
O God of the universe, and our joy,
   happy are all who trust you.

(Inspired by Psalm 84)

UPPER LEFT: *Side Billabong, East Alligator Valley*
LOWER LEFT: *Lotus Lily beside Walkarr Billabong*
RIGHT: *Magela Creek Lilies*

LEFT: *Lilies, post-wet season, Buywek Goluy Billabong*
RIGHT: *Twin Falls (Gungurdul)*

MANY WITNESSES

O give thanks to the Lord
for he is good,

    His love endures for ever!

Let the beauties of Yellow Waters
bear witness,
let the reflections of the South Alligator
portray it:

    His love endures for ever!

Come, bushland around Jabiru,
tell your secret.
Come, wind through pandanus forest,
whisper your joy.
Water streamers of Jim Jim,
insist on it.
Roaring voice of Twin Falls,
declare it:

    His love endures for ever!

Storms over the peaks of Koongarra,
thunder it.
Lightning over Mt Brockman,
signal it.
Spread the good news, Magela
in wide flood.
Woo us with the beautiful truth,
billabongs of Cannon Hill:

    His love endures for ever!

Let every tourist and ranger,
fisherman and hiker,
let traditional owner
and visiting schoolchildren,
join in a flood of gratitude
and sing for joy:

    His love endures for ever!

NOURLANGIE SUNSET

It was a simple evening meal —
just sandwiches and soft drink.
But under the paper barks
beside Anbangbang Billabong
it was something else.

We looked across watery lily fields
with an occasional white flower.
A family of wild geese
flew off in a flurry.
Two brown ducks
and some stately egrets
watched us warily,
but fed on.

Over the lone mangrove clump
rose great Nourlangie Rock;
when the setting sun
broke briefly through
funereal clouds,
it bathed the old rock face
of many dreamings
with glorious red ochre.

It was a simple meal
under the paper barks.
But it tasted
like sacrament.

UPPER LEFT: *Magpie Goose in flight*
LOWER LEFT: *Magpie Geese, late dry season*
RIGHT: *Nourlangie Rock (Burrungguy) from Anbangbang Billabong*

LIKE MANNA

Entranced
at sweet-sour dusk,
we watch the west
where wild geese fly
in restless quest.

Briefly
we savour a joy
which cannot be stored,
but, like true manna,
its Source adored.

LEFT: *Magpie Geese and Jabiru*
RIGHT: *Geese of Umuwal, East Alligator River*

SHIFTING CAMP

When I leave
this life, Lord,
as a traveller shifting camp,
I will trust your word:
    Eye has not seen
    nor ear heard
    what you have yet
    in store.
But of one thing
I am sure:
    Trailing clouds of glory
    will I come
    from this world,
    my first, fair home.

UPPER LEFT: *Two-lined Dragon*
LOWER LEFT: *Chestnut-quilled Rock-Pigeon*
(Gurrbelak)
UPPER RIGHT: Barringtonia *flowers, East*
Alligator Floodplain
LOWER RIGHT: *Lightning Dreaming*
(Namarrkurn)

Gulungul Creek

To
LINDA
from
Stu
Woodlake Books
Sept. 8/1993